The Orphan of China

Voltaire

Translation by William F. Fleming

To the Most Noble Duke of Richelieu, Marshal and Peer of France, First Gentleman of the Chamber to His Majesty, Governor of Languedoc, and Member of the Academy of Sciences.

Contents

Dramatis Personæ

Genghis Khan, Emperor of the Tartars.
Octar, Officers under Genghis Khan.
Osman, Officers under Genghis Khan.
Zamti, a learned Mandarin.
Idame, wife of Zamti.
Asseli, friend to Idame.
Etan, friend to Zamti.

This piece was produced in Paris, 1755, when the author was in exile.

To the most noble Duke of Richelieu, Marshal and Peer of France, First Gentleman of the Chamber to his Majesty, Governor of Languedoc, and Member of the Academy of Sciences.

My Lord, I would have presented you with a piece of fine marble; but, instead of it, can only offer you a few Chinese figures. This little performance is not indeed worthy of your acceptance; there is no hero in this piece, who has united all parties in his favor, and rendered himself universally agreeable, by the force of superior talents, or supported a falling kingdom, or made the noble attempt to overthrow an English colony with four cannons only. I know better than anybody else the insignificance of my own works; but everything may be forgiven to an attachment of forty years' standing. The world, indeed, will say, that, retired as I am to the foot of the Alps, covered with eternal snows, and where I ought to be nothing but a philosopher, I had still vanity enough to let it be known, that France's brightest ornament on the banks of the Seine has not forgotten me. I have consulted my own heart alone, which has always guided me, inspired every word, and directed every action. You know it has sometimes deceived me; but not after such long and convincing proofs. If this tragedy should survive its author, permit it to inform posterity, that he who wrote it was honored with your friendship; that your uncle laid the foundation of the fine arts in France, and that you supported them in their decline.

I took the first hint of this tragedy some time since from reading the "Orphan of Tchao," a Chinese tragedy, translated by Father Bremare, an account of which is given in Du Halde's history. This piece was written in the fourteenth century, and under the dynasty of Genghis Khan; an additional proof, that the Tartar conquerors did not change the manners of the conquered nation; on the other hand, they protected and encouraged all the arts established in China, and adopted their laws: an extraordinary instance of the natural superiority which reason and genius have over blind force and barbarism. Twice have the Tartars acted in this manner; for when they had once more subdued this great empire, the beginning of last century, they submitted a second time to the wisdom of the conquered, and the two nations formed but one people, governed by the most ancient laws in the world; a most remarkable event, the illustration of which was the principal end of this performance.

The Chinese tragedy, which they call "The Orphan," was taken out of an immense collection of the theatrical performances of that nation, which has cultivated this art for about three thousand years before it was invented by the Greeks, the art of making living portraits of the actions of men, establishing schools of morality, and teaching virtue in dialogue and representation. For a long time dramatic poetry was held in esteem only in that vast country of China, separated from and unknown to the rest of the world, and in the city of Athens. Rome was unacquainted with it till above four hundred years afterwards. If you look for it among the Persians, or Indians, who pass for an inventive people, you will not find it there; it has never yet reached them. Asia was contented with the fables of Palpay and Lokman, which contain all their morality, and have instructed by their allegories every age and nation.

One would have imagined, that from making animals speak, there was but one step to make men speak also, to introduce them on the stage, and to form the dramatic art; and yet this ingenious people never thought of it: from whence we may infer, that the Chinese, Greeks, and Romans are the only ancient nations, who were acquainted with the true spirit of society. Nothing indeed renders men more sociable, polishes their manners, or improves their reason more than the assembling them together for the mutual enjoyment of intellectual pleasure. Scarce had Peter the Great polished Russia before theatres were established there. The more Germany improves, the more of our dramatic representations has it adopted. Those few places where they were not received in the last age are never ranked amongst the civilized countries.

The "Orphan of Tchao" is a valuable monument of antiquity, and gives us more insight into the manners of China than all the histories which ever were, or ever will be written of that vast empire. 'Tis true, indeed, it is extremely barbarous, when compared with the excellent performances of our times; but, notwithstanding, is a masterpiece, when placed in competition with the pieces written by our authors in the fourteenth century. Our "Troubadours," "Bazoche," the company of "Children Without Care," and "The Foolish Mother," all of them fall short of the Chinese author. It is remarkable also, that this piece is written in the language of the Mandarins, which has never changed, whilst we can scarce understand the language that was spoken in the time of Louis XII. and Charles VIII.

One can only compare the "Orphan of Tchao" to the English and Spanish tragedies of the sixteenth century, which still please beyond sea, and on the other side of the Pyrenees. The action lasts five and twenty years, as in some of the monstrous farces of Shakespeare and Lope de Vega, which are called tragedies, though they are nothing but a heap of incredible stories. The enemy of the house of Tchao wants to destroy the head of it; and for that purpose lets loose on him a great dog, whom he imagines endowed with the power of discovering guilt by instinct, as James Aimar amongst us was said to have found out thieves by his wand: at last he forges an order from the emperor, and sends his enemy Tchao a rope, a dagger, and some poison. Tchao sings, according to the custom of his country, and very deliberately cuts his own throat, in consequence of that obedience, which every man owes to the divine right of the emperor of China. The persecutor puts to death three hundred persons of the family of Tchao. The prince's widow is brought to bed of the orphan. The infant is saved from the rage of the tyrant, who had exterminated the whole family, and would have destroyed the only remaining branch of it: the tyrant orders all the children in all the towns round about to be destroyed, in hopes that the orphan might perish amongst the rest in the general slaughter.

We fancy we are reading the Arabian Night's Entertainment put into scenes; and yet, in spite of all these marvellous and improbable things, it is extremely interesting: though there is such a multiplicity of events, all is clear and simple; a merit which must recommend it to every age and nation, and which is greatly wanting in our modern performances. The Chinese piece is indeed very deficient with regard to all other beauties: there is no unity of time or action, no picture of the manners; no sentiment, eloquence, reason or passion in it; and yet, as I said before, the work is superior to anything we could produce in former ages.

How comes it to pass, that the Chinese, who in the fourteenth century, and a long time before, could boast of better dramatic performances than any European nation, still remain, as it were, in the infancy of this art, while we, in process of time, and by dint of pains and assiduity, have been able to produce about a dozen pieces, which, if they are not absolutely perfect, are at least much above anything the rest of the world could ever pretend to of this kind. The Chinese, as well as the rest of the Asiatics, have stopped at the first elements of poetry, eloquence, natural philosophy, astronomy, and painting; all practised by them so long before they were known to us. They began in everything much sooner than us, but made no progress afterwards; like the ancient Egyptians, who first taught the Greeks, and became at last so ignorant, as not even to be capable of receiving instruction from them.

These people, whom we take so much pains and go so far to visit; from whom, with the utmost difficulty, we have obtained permission to carry the riches of Europe, and to instruct them, do not to this day know how much we are their superiors; they are not even far enough advanced in knowledge to venture to imitate us, and don't so much as know whether we have any history or not.

The celebrated Metastasio has made choice of pretty nearly the same subject as myself for one of his dramatic poems, an orphan escaped from the destruction of his family, and has drawn his plot from a dynasty nine hundred years before our era.

The Chinese tragedy of the "Orphan of Tchao" differs in many respects; and I have chosen one that is not much like either of them, except in the name, as I have confined my plan to the grand epoch of Genghis Khan. I have endeavored to describe the manners of the Tartars and Chinese: the most interesting events are nothing when they do not paint the manners; and this painting, which is one of the greatest secrets of the art, is no more than an idle amusement, when it does not tend to inspire notions of honor and virtue.

I will venture to say, that from the "Henriade" to the publication of "Zaïre," and this tragedy, be it good or bad, such is the principle by which I have always been governed; and that in my history of the age of Louis XIV., I have celebrated both my king and country, without flattery to either. In labors of this kind I have spent above forty years of my life. But observe the following words of a Chinese author, translated into Spanish by the famous Navarrete.

"When you compose any work, show it only to your friends; dread the public, and your brother writers; for they will play false with you, abuse everything you do, and impute to you what you never did: calumny with her hundred trumpets, will sound them all to your destruction; whilst truth, who is dumb, shall remain with you. The celebrated Ming was accused of hating Tien and Li, and the Emperor Vang: when the old man died, they found amongst his papers a panegyric on Vang, a hymn to Tien, another to Li, etc."

Voltaire.

ACT I

SCENE I

Scene a Mandarin's palace near the court, in the city of Cambalu, now called Pekin.

Idame, Asseli

Idame: O Asseli, amidst this scene of horror, Whilst desolation rages through the land, And the proud Tartar threatens instant ruin To this devoted palace, must thy friend Experience new calamities?

Asseli: Alas! We all partake the general ruin; all Must with the public sorrows mix our own: Who doth not tremble for a father's life, A husband's, son's, or brother's? even within These sacred walls, where dwells the holy band, The ministers of heaven, the interpreters Of China's laws, with helpless infancy, And feeble age; even here we are not safe: Who knows how far the cruel conqueror May urge his triumphs, whilst the thunder breaks On every side, and soon may burst upon us?

Idame: Who is this great destroyer, this dire scourge Of Catai's sinking empire?

Asseli: He is called The king of kings, the fiery Genghis Khan, Who lays the fertile fields of Asia waste, And makes it but a monument of ruin: Already Octar, his successful chief, Has stormed the palace; this once powerful empire, The mistress of the world, is bathed in blood!

Idame: Knowest thou, my friend, that this destructive tyrant, Whom now we tremble at, who proudly thus Treads on the necks of kings, is yet no more Than a wild Scythian soldier; bred to arms And practised in the trade of blood; who long Had wandered o'er the neighboring deserts, there Formed a rude band of lawless rioters, And fought his way to glory; now successful, And now oppressed, at length by fortune led Hither he came for refuge: Asseli, I think thou must remember him, his name Was Temugin

Asseli: Ha! he who once addressed His vows to thee! thy angry father then Rejected him with scorn; though now his name Is grown so terrible

Idame: It is the same: Methought even then I saw the rising dawn Of future glory: I remember well, Even when he came a beggar to the palace, And craved protection, he behaved like one Born to command: he loved me; and I own My foolish heart had well nigh listened to him: Perhaps it soothed the woman's vanity To hold this lion in my toils; perhaps I hoped in time to soften his rude soul, And bend his savage fierceness to the ways Of social life: he might have served the state Which now he would destroy: our proud refusal Incensed the hero, fatal may it prove To this unhappy kingdom: well thou knowest Our pride and jealousy: the ancient laws Of this imperial city; our religion, Our interest and our glory, all forbid Alliance with the nations: for myself, The noble Zamti merited my love, And heaven hath joined me to him by the ties Of holy marriage: who would e'er have thought This poor despised abandoned Scythian thus Should triumph over us? I refused his hand; I am a wife and mother; how that thought Alarms me! he is fiery and revengeful; A Scythian never pardons: cruel fate! And will this valiant nation tamely yield Its neck to slavery, and be led like sheep To slaughter?

Asseli: 'Tis reported the Koreans Have raised an army, but we know not yet If it be true

Idame: This sad uncertainty But doubles our distress: heaven only knows What we must suffer, if the emperor Has found a place of refuge, if the queen Is fallen beneath the tyrant's power, if yet They live; alas! the last surviving pledge Of their unhappy nuptials, the dear infant Entrusted to our care! I tremble for him Perhaps my Zamti's sacred character And holy office may subdue the hearts Of these proud conquerors; savage as they are, And thirsting for the blood of half mankind, They yet believe there is a power above That rules o'er all; nature in every breast Hath wisely stamped the image of its God: I talk of hope, but have a thousand fears That wring my heart

SCENE II

Idame, Zamti, Asseli

Asseli: O my unhappy lord, Speak, what must be our fate? is it determined? What hast thou seen?

Zamti: I tremble to repeat it: We are undone: our empire is no more; A prey to robbers: what hath it availed us That we have trod in the fair paths of virtue? Long time secure within the arms of peace We shone illustrious in the rolls of time, And gave a bright example to mankind: From us the world received its laws; but vain Is human worth when lawless power prevails: I saw the northern hive rush in upon us, And force their passage through a sea of blood; Where'er they passed they spread destruction round them: At length they seized the palace, where the best Of sovereigns and of men, with calm composure And resignation yielded to his fate: The wretched queen lay fainting in his arms: Those of their numerous sons, whom lusty manhood Had sent to battle, were already slain: The rest, who naught could give him but their tears, Hung at his knees and wept; by secret paths I found an entrance to the palace; there Did I behold the cruel tyrants bind In ignominious chains the conquered king, His children, and his wife

Idame: Unhappy monarch! O what a change is this! relentless heaven!

Zamti: The wretched captive turned his eyes towards me, And in the sacred language, to the Tartar And to the multitude unknown, cried out, "Preserve my last and only hope—my son." From my full heart I promised, swore to act As he directed me, then fled to thee Whether the tyrants, busied in their search Of plunder, thought not of me, or the symbol Which here I wear of the divinity Struck their rude souls with reverential awe, Or whether heaven in kind compassion meant To save my precious charge, and cast a cloud O'er their deluded eyes, I know not what Drew their attention, but they let me pass

Idame: We yet may save him, he shall go with me, And with my son; old Etan shall conduct us: In some lone wood, or solitary cave, We may conceal him till the search is past: Thank heaven they have not reached us yet

Zamti: Alas! No place is sacred, no asylum's left For the dear royal infant: I expect The brave Koreans, but they'll come too late: But let us seize the favorable hour, And lodge our precious pledge in safety

SCENE III

Zamti, Idame, Asseli, Etan

Zamti: Etan, Thou seemest disordered: what's the news?

Idame: My lord, We must away; the Scythian has prevailed, And all is lost

Etan: You are observed, and flight Is now impossible: a guard is placed Around us: all obey the conqueror, And tremble at his power: the emperor's loss Fills every heart with terror

Zamti: Is he dead?

Idame: O heaven!

Etan: It was indeed a dreadful sight: Himself, his queen, his children, butchered all; A race divine, respected, loved, adored; Their headless trunks exposed to the derision Of their proud conqueror, whilst their trembling subjects Submissive bend beneath the yoke, nor dare To shed a tear o'er those whom long they loved At length our haughty lord, grown tired of conquest, And satiated with blood, proclaimed to all The terms of life, eternal slavery This northern tyrant, whom the wrath of heaven Hath sent for our destruction, once contemned And spurned at by our court, returns to glut His vengeance on us: these wild sons of rapine, Who live in tents, in chariots, and in fields, Will never brook confinement 'midst the walls Of this close city: they detest our arts, Our customs, and our laws; and therefore mean To change them all; to make this splendid seat Of empire one vast desert, like their own

Idame: I know the conqueror comes to sate his vengeance On this unhappy kingdom: whilst I lived Unnoticed and obscure, I might have hope Of safety; but that hope is now no more: The night is past that hid me from the eye Of persecution, and I must be wretched Thrice happy those, who to a tyrant master Are still unknown

Zamti: Who knows but gracious heaven May interpose and save the royal infant: 'Tis our first duty to preserve the charge Committed to our care, and guard him well What comes this Tartar for?

Idame: O heaven! defend us,

SCENE IV

Octar: Hear, slaves; and let your answer be—obedience: An infant yet remains, of royal race, Amongst you: in the conqueror's name I here Command you to deliver him—to me I shall expect him here: begone; delay Were dangerous: bring him instantly, or know, Destruction waits on all, but first on you The day's far spent; ere night he must be found: Remember, and obey

SCENE V

Zamti, Idame

Idame: O dreadful message! For what are we reserved? Alas! my lord, Ne'er till this day of blood did crimes like this Affright my soul: you answer not, but send Your fruitless sighs to heaven. Sweet innocent, Must we then give thee up a sacrifice To brutal rage?

Zamti: I've promised, sworn to save him

Idame: What can thy oaths, thy promises avail? Thou canst not keep them; every hope is lost

Zamti: And wouldst thou have me sacrifice the son Of my loved sovereign?

Idame: O I cannot bear To think of it; my eyes are bathed in tears O were I not a mother, would kind heaven But grant me now to shorten my sad days, Then would I say to Zamti, come, my lord, We'll die together; all is lost to us, And we will perish with our country

Zamti: Who That sees the wretched fate of Cathay's kings Would wish to live? what is this phantom death, That thus appalls mankind? the wretch's hope, The villain's terror, and the brave man's scorn: Without reluctance, and without regret, The wise expect and meet him as a friend

Idame: What secret purpose labors in your breast? Your cheek is pale, your eyes are filled with tears; My sympathizing heart feels all your sorrows, And would relieve them; what have you resolved?

Zamti: To keep my oath; therefore away, and watch The royal infant: I shall follow you

Idame: Alas! a woman's tears can ne'er defend him

SCENE VI

Zamti, Etan

Zamti: Vain is your care, your kind compassion vain, For he must die; the nation's weal demands it Think rather how thou mayest preserve thy country

Zamti: Yes, I will make the dreadful sacrifice Etan, I know thou holdest this empire dear; Yes, thou adorest the God of heaven and earth, As worshipped by our ancestors; that God Our bonzes know not, and our tyrants scorn

Etan: In him I trust, on him alone rely For my own comfort, and my country's safety

Zamti: Swear then by him, and his all-ruling power, That thou wilt bury in eternal silence The solemn secret that I mean to pour Into thy faithful bosom: swear, thy hand Shall still be ready to perform whate'er Thy duty and thy God by me command

Etan: I swear; and may the miseries that have fallen On this unhappy kingdom light on me, If ever I am false in word or deed!

Zamti: I cannot now recede: then mark me, Etan

Etan: Alas! thou weepest: amidst the general ruin Can there be cause for added grief?

Zamti: The doom Is past, my friend, and cannot be reversed

Etan: I know it cannot; but a stranger's son—

Zamti: A stranger! he, my king!

Etan: When I remember He is our emperor's child, I shudder at it: What's to be done?

Zamti: My path thou seest, is here Prescribed, and every action noted down By our new tyrants; thou mayest act with freedom, Because unknown and unobserved: thou knowest The orphan's place of refuge: for a time We may conceal him 'midst the secret tombs Of our great ancestors; then shelter him Beneath Korea's chief; he will protect The royal infant: leave the rest to me

Etan: And how will you appear without him, how Appease the conqueror?

Zamti: I have wherewithal To glut his vengeance

Etan: You, my lord?

Zamti: O nature! O cruel duty!

Etan: How—

Zamti: I have a son, An only child, now in his cradle—go And seize him

Etan: Ha! your son!

Zamti: To save—my king Away, and let him—but I can no more

Etan: Alas! my lord, what a command is this! I never can obey it

Zamti: Think on Zamti; Think on his love, his weakness, his misfortunes, Thy duty, and—thy oath

Etan: 'Twas rash and vain: Thou didst extort it from me: I admire Thy generous purpose; but if as a friend I might be heard—

Zamti: No more; I've heard too much Already: what is all that thou couldst say To what a father feels? When nature's silenced, Friendship should urge no longer

Etan: I obey

Zamti: Leave me for pity's sake

SCENE VIII

Zamti: [Alone.] Is nature silent? O wretched father! still thou hearest that voice So fatal and so dear: O drown it, heaven, In sweet oblivion; do not let my wife And her dear babe distract this heart; O heal My wounded heart: but man is far too weak To conquer nature: let thy aid divine Support me, and assist my feeble virtue!

ACT II

SCENE I

Zamti: [Alone.] This tardy Etan, wherefore comes he not To tell me—what I dread to hear? perhaps Ere this the dreadful sacrifice is past: I had not power to offer it myself O my dear child, how shall I ask my friend The horrid question, how conceal my grief?

SCENE II

Zamti, Etan

Zamti: I see 'tis done; I know it by thy tears; They speak too plainly

Etan: Thy unhappy son—

Zamti: No more of that: speak of our empire's hope, The royal infant; is he safe?

Etan: He is: Within the tombs of his great ancestors Concealed from every eye; to you he owes A life begun in misery, perhaps A fatal gift

Zamti: It is enough, he lives O you, to whom I pay this cruel duty, Forgive a father's tears

Etan: Alas! my lord, You must not give away to sorrow here: 'Tis dangerous even to weep

Zamti: And whither, Etan, Must I transport my griefs? how bear the cries, The bitter anguish, the despair, the rage, The execrations of a frantic mother? May we not yet deceive her for a time?

Etan: We seized him in her absence, and I flew To guard the orphan king

Zamti: A while, my friend, We might impose on her credulity Couldst thou not say we had delivered up The royal orphan, and concealed her son In safety? Truth is often most destructive, And still we love it, though it makes us wretched Come, Etan, let us home—O heaven! she's here! Observe her, what despair and terror dwell On her pale cheek!

SCENE III

Zamti, Idame

Idame: Barbarian, can it be? Could Zamti e'er command it? could he offer The dreadful sacrifice? I'll not believe it: Thou couldst not be more cruel than the laws Of our proud conquerors, or the Tartar's sword Alas! thou weepest

Zamti: Thou too must weep with Zamti But thou must join with him to save thy king

Idame: What! sacrifice my child!

Zamti: It must be so: Thou wert a subject ere thou wert a mother

Idame: Has nature then lost all her influence o'er A father's heart?

Zamti: She has too much; but ne'er Shall thwart my duty

Idame: 'Tis a barbarous virtue, And I abhor it: I have seen, like thee, Our empire lost, and wept our sovereign's fate; But why pour forth an infant's guiltless blood, Yet undemanded; why revere as gods Your sleeping kings, that moulder in the tomb? Hath Zamti sworn to them that he would kill His darling child? alas! the rich and poor, The monarch and the slave, are equal all By nature; all alike to sorrow born, Each has his share; and in the general wreck, All duty bids us is—to save our own O had I fallen into the snare, and staid A moment longer with the royal orphan, My child had fallen into the cruel hands Of ruffians; but I would have perished with him Nature and love recalled me, and I snatched My lovely infant from the ravishers, Preserved the son and mother; saved even thee, Thou barbarous father

Zamti: Doth my son then live?

Idame: He doth; and thou shouldst bend to gracious heaven For goodness thus unmerited: repent, And be a father

Zamti: O almighty power, Forgive the joy that, spite of all my firmness, Thus mingles with my tears: alas! my love, Vain are our hopes of happiness, and vain Thy fond endeavors to prolong the life Of our dear infant; these inhuman tyrants Will force him from us; he must yield to fate

Idame: But hear me, dearest Zamti.

Zamti: He must die

Idame: Barbarian, stay, and tremble at the rage Of an afflicted desperate mother

Zamti: I Shall do my duty, you may give up yours, And sacrifice your husband to the foe: This is a day of blood; let Zamti join His murdered king, and perish with his country

Idame: What is your country, what your king to me? The name of subject is not half so sacred As husband or as father. Love and nature Are heaven's first great unalterable laws, And cannot be reversed: the rest are all From mortal man, and may be changed at pleasure Would I could save the royal heir, but not By the much dearer blood of Zamti's son! Pity a wretched mother; on my knees I beg thee, cruel Zamti: O remember For whom I slighted this proud conqueror, This mighty warrior; was it not for thee? And wilt thou not protect my son, not hear The voice of nature pleading for thy child?

Zamti: It is too much: thou dost abuse the power Which love has given thee o'er thy Zamti's heart: Couldst thou but see—

Idame: I own, my lord, I feel A mother's weakness, and a mother's sorrows; Yet may I boast a heart as firm as thine; Away, and lead me on to death: I'm ready To perish for my son

Zamti: I know thy virtues

SCENE IV

Zamti, Idame, Octar

Octar: Where are these traitors? why are my commands Thus disobeyed? what have ye done with him, The orphan prince? guards, bring him to our presence, The emperor approaches; let him see The victim at his feet: you, soldiers, watch These rebels

Zamti: I obey, my lord, the orphan Shall be delivered up

Idame: 'Tis false; he shall not: I'll sooner lose my life than part with him

Octar: Guards, take this woman hence: the emperor comes

SCENE V

Genghis, Octar, Osman

Genghis: At length, my friends, 'tis time to sheathe the sword, And let the vanquished breathe; I've spread destruction And terror through the land, but I will give The nation peace: the royal infant's death Shall satisfy my wrath; with him shall rot The seeds of foul rebellion; all the plots, Feuds and divisions, fears and jealousies, That whilst the phantom of a royal heir Subsists, must disunite us, he alone Of all the hated race remains, and he Shall follow them: henceforth we will not raze Their boasted works, their monuments of art, Their sacred laws; for sacred they esteem The musty rolls, which superstition taught Their ancestors to worship: be it so, The error may be useful, it employs The people, and may make them more obedient [To Octar] Octar, to thee I shall commit the power, To bear my standard to the western world [To another officer] Rule thou in conquered India, and interpret Thy sovereign's great decrees; from Samarcand To Tanais' borders, I shall send my sons Away—stay, Octar

SCENE VI

Genghis, Octar

Genghis: Couldst thou e'er have thought Fortune would raise me to this height of glory? That I should reign supreme, and triumph here, Even in this palace, where disgraced and wretched I sought in vain for refuge, and was treated With insolence and scorn: the proud possessors Of this unconquered empire then disdained A Scythian, and a haughty fair refused That hand which now directs the fate of millions

Octar: Amidst this scene of glory, how, my lord, Can thoughts like these disturb you?

Genghis: Still the wrongs I suffered in adversity oppress me: I own the weakness of my foolish heart, And hoped to find that happiness in love, Which glory, wealth, and empire, cannot give It hurts my pride to think how I was spurned By that contemptuous woman; she shall know, At least, and see the object of her scorn To have her mourn the honors that she lost In losing Genghis will be some revenge

Octar: The shouts of victory, and the voice of fame, Have been so long familiar to my ears, That I have little relish for the plaints Of whining love

Genghis: Nor has thy friend indulged That fatal passion since her proud refusal: I own the fair Idame won my heart, By charms unknown before: our barren deserts Could never produce a face like hers, a mind So formed to please; her every motion fired My captive soul, but her imprudent scorn Restored my freedom; nobler objects claim A monarch's care; I'll think no more of her, Let her repent at leisure of her pride Octar, I charge thee, talk not of Idame.

Octar: You have, indeed, affairs of greater moment That call for your attention

Genghis: Then farewell To love, and all its follies

SCENE VII

Genghis, Octar, Osman

Osman: O my lord, The victim was prepared, the guard was ranged On every side, when (wonderful to tell!) A strange event perplexed us all.—A woman Of frantic mien, with wild dishevelled hair, And bathed in tears, rushed in upon us; "stop," Aloud she cried, "inhuman ruffians, stop, It is my son, you've been deceived; 'tis not The emperor's child, but mine:" her eyes, her voice, Her fury, her despair, her every gesture, Was nature's language all, and spoke the mother: When lo! her husband came, with downcast eyes And gloomy aspect; sullenly he cried, "This is the royal orphan, this the blood, Which you demanded, take it:" as he spake, Fast flowed his tears. The wretched matron, pale And motionless awhile, as struck with death, Fell prostrate; then, long as her faltering voice Could utter the imperfect sound, cried out, "Give me my son:" her sorrows were sincere, Never was grief more bitter, doubts arose Amongst us, and I came to know your orders

Genghis: If 'tis the work of art, I will explore The mystery soon, and woe to the deceivers: Think they to cast a veil before my eyes, And mock their sovereign? let them if they dare

Octar: My lord, this woman never can deceive us; The emperor's son was placed beneath her care; A master's child might easily attract The faithful servant's love, and danger make The charge more precious still; the ties of nature Are not more strong than those of fantasy: But we shall soon unravel it

Genghis: Who is This woman?

Octar: Wife of a proud Mandarin: One of those lettered sages who defy The power of kings; a numerous band! but now, Thank heaven, reduced by thy victorious arms To slavery: Zamti is the traitor's name Who watches o'er the victim

Genghis: Go, my Octar, Interrogate this guilty pair, and learn, If possible, the truth: let all our guards Be ready at their posts: they talk, it seems, Of a surprise that the Koreans mean To march against us on the river's bank: An army hath been seen: we soon shall know What bold adventurers are so fond of death, To court destruction from the sons of war, And force them to depopulate the world

ACT III

SCENE I

Genghis, Octar, Osman, Attendants

Genghis: What say the captives, is the fraud discovered, And vengeance taken on these vile impostors? Have they delivered up the orphan prince To Octar?

Osman: Prayers, and threats, and torments, all Are vain: the undaunted Zamti still persists In his first answer: on his open brows Are engraved the marks of truth: the mournful fair one, Whose grief but adds new lustre to her charms, With tears incessant and heart-rending sighs, Moves every heart: spite of ourselves we wept Her wretched fate: ne'er did my eyes behold A sweeter mourner: she entreats to see And speak with you; the conqueror of kings, She hopes, will hear the wretched, and in wrath Remember mercy; that he will protect A guiltless child, and show mankind his goodness Is like his power, unlimited. 'Twas thus, My lord, she spoke of you, and I have promised She shall have audience

Genghis: [To one of the attendants] Bid her enter now, We shall unravel this deep mystery; But let her not imagine a few sighs, And bidden tears, can e'er impose on me: I have experienced all these female arts, But I defy them now: let her be careful, Her life depends on her sincerity

Osman: My lord, she comes

Genghis: What do I see? O heaven! It cannot be Idame, sure my senses—

SCENE II

Genghis, Idame, Octar, Osman, Guards

Idame: My lord, I came not to solicit pardon, My forfeit life is yours, I ask not for it: Why should I wish for years of added woe? But spare a guiltless infant

Genghis: Rise, Idame, Fate conquers all, it has deceived us both If heaven hath raised a poor inhabitant Of Scythia, once the object of your scorn, To power, and splendor, you have naught to fear: The emperor never will avenge the wrongs Of Temugin; but public good demands The royal victim; 'tis a sacrifice Which must be made: for your own son, myself Will be his guard: I promise to protect him

Idame: Then I am happy

Genghis: But inform me, madam, What is this fraud, this mystery between you? For I must know it all

Idame: O spare the wretched

Genghis: Have I not cause to hate this Zamti? **Idame:** You, My lord?

Genghis: I've said too much

Idame: Restore my child, You've promised it

Genghis: His pardon must depend On you alone: you know I have been injured, My favors scorned, my orders disobeyed: Who is this Zamti, this respected lord, This husband? in that name alone comprised Is every guilt: what charms has he to boast Who braves me thus?

Idame: He was my only comfort, My joy, my happiness, the best of men; He served his God, his country, and his king

Genghis: How long, Idame, have you been united?

Idame: Ever since the fatal time, when wayward fortune Espoused thy cause, and gave a tyrant power To scourge mankind

Genghis: I understand you, madam, E'er since the time you mean, when I was scorned By a proud beauty, when this country first Deserved the chains which it was doomed to wear

SCENE III

Genghis, Octar, Osman

[On one side of the stage Idame, and Zamti On the other, Guards.]

Genghis: What sayest thou, slave? hast thou delivered up The emperor's son?

Zamti: I have, my lord, 'tis done: I have fulfilled my duty

Genghis: Well thou knowest Nor fraud, nor insolence escape my vengeance: If thou hast dared to hide him from my wrath, He must be found, his death shall follow thine [To the guards] Seize and destroy that infant

Zamti: Wretched father! **Idame**: Stay, cruel tyrant, stay, is this your pity, Is this your promise?

Genghis: I have been deceived; Explain the mystery, madam, or he dies

Idame: I'll tell thee all; and if it be a crime To follow nature, and obey her laws, If still thy cruel spirit thirsts for blood, Let all your anger light on me, but spare The noble Zamti: to our mutual care The emperor entrusted his dear son: Thou knowest too well what scenes of horrid slaughter Followed thy cruel victory, and marked Thy steps with blood; that might have satisfied A less inhuman conqueror: when thy slaves Demanded our last hope, the royal heir, My generous Zamti, faithful to his king, To duty gave up all, and sacrificed His son, nor listened to the powerful voice Of nature; I admired that patriot firmness I had not strength to imitate: alas! I am a mother, how could I consent To my child's death? my terrors, my despair, My rage, my anguish, all too plainly spoke What Zamti strove to hide: behold, my lord, The wretched father, he deserves your pity: So does my guiltless infant: punish me, And me alone: forgive me, dearest Zamti, Forgive a mother's tenderness, forgive A wife that loves thee and would save thy son

Zamti: I have forgiven thee, and, thank heaven, my king, The royal infant's safe

Genghis: 'Tis false; begone, And find him, traitor, or thou diest; atone For thy past crimes

Zamti: The crime were to obey A tyrant, but my royal master's voice Cries from the tomb, and bids me tell thee, Genghis, Thou art my conqueror, but not my king: Were Zamti born thy subject, he had been Most faithful to thee: I have sacrificed My son, and thinkest thou I can fear to die?

Genghis: [To the guard] Away with him

Idame: O stay

Genghis: I'll hear no more

Idame: I have deserved thy anger, I alone Should feel thy vengeance: thou hast slain my king, And now my husband and my child must fall By thy destructive hand: inhuman tyrant, When will thy wrath be satisfied?

Genghis: Away: Follow thy guilty husband: darest thou plead For mercy, thou reproach me?

Idame: Then all hope Is lost

Genghis: If ever I think of clemency, It must not be till ample reparation Is made for all my wrongs: you understand me

SCENE IV

Genghis, Octar

Genghis: What means this fluttering heart, and wherefore thus Steals from my breast the involuntary sigh? Some power divine protects her: O my Octar, What secret charms have innocence and beauty, That proud authority should thus submit To own their influence? I have lost myself And want a friend; O lend me thy kind counsel

Octar: Since I must speak, I'll speak with freedom; know then This dangerous branch of a detested race Must be cut off, or we are not secure In our new conquest; victory's best guard Is rigor; by severity alone Your power can be established. Time, my lord, Will bring back order and tranquillity; The people by degrees forget their wrongs, Or pardon them: you then may reign in peace

Genghis: And can it be Idame, that proud beauty, Given to another, to my mortal foe! **Octar:** She merits not your pity, but your hate; I cannot, must not think you ever loved her; 'Twas but a short and momentary flame, That sparkled and expired; her cruel scorn, Her proud refusal, and the hand of time, Have quite extinguished it; she is no more To Genghis now than the ignoble wife, Of an abandoned traitor

Genghis: He shall die; A slave! a rival!

Octar: Wherefore lives he yet? Strike, and revenge thyself

Genghis: I know not why, But my fond heart still trembles at the thought Of injuring her: subdued by beauty's tears I dare not hurt a rival and a slave; Even in the husband I respect the wife: Is love indeed so great a conqueror, And must I grace his triumphs?

Octar: All I know, And all I wish for, is to follow thee, The rattling chariot, and the sounding bow, The fiery coursers, and the din of arms: These are my passions, these the joys of Octar: I am a stranger to the sighs of love, And think them far beneath the royal soul Of Genghis; they debase a character So great as thine

Genghis: I know my power, I know That I could make her mine: but what avails The fairest form without the conquered heart? Where is the joy to press within our arms A trembling slave? to see her beauteous eyes Forever bathed in tears, and her full heart Oppressed with sorrow? 'tis a barbarous triumph: The savage herd, that through the forest roam, Enjoy more peace, and boast a purer love: The fair Idame has some secret power That charms me more than victory and empire: I thought I could have driven her from my heart, But she returns, and triumphs

SCENE V

Genghis, Octar, Osman

Genghis: Well: what says she?

Osman: That she will perish with her husband rather Than tell the place where, hid from every eye, The orphan lies concealed; the tender husband Supports her in his arms; with added courage Inspires her soul, and teaches her to die They wish to be united in the grave; The people throng around, and every eye Is wet with tears, lamenting their sad fate

Genghis: And does Idame talk of death from me? Fly, Osman, fly, tell her I hold her life As sacred as my own: away

SCENE VI

Genghis, Octar

Octar: This infant, Concerning him, my lord—what's to be done?

Genghis: Nothing

Octar: You gave commands he should be torn Even from Idame's bosom

Genghis: We must think Of that hereafter

Octar: What if they should hide—

Genghis: He cannot escape us

Octar: Still they may deceive you

Genghis: Idame is incapable of fraud

Octar: And would you then preserve the royal race?

Genghis: I would preserve Idame; for the rest 'Tis equal all, dispose it as thou wilt Go, bring her hither—stay—my Octar—try If thou canst soften this rebellious slave, This Zamti, and persuade him to obey me We will not heed this infant; he shall make me A nobler sacrifice

Octar: Who, he, my lord?

Genghis: Ay, he

Octar: What hopest thou?

Genghis: To subdue Idame, To see her, to adore her, to be loved By that ungrateful fair one; or to take My full revenge, to punish her, and die

ACT IV

SCENE I

Genghis: [A troop of Tartar soldiers] Are these my promised joys? is this the fruit Of all my labors? where's the liberty, The rest I hoped for? I but feel the weight Without the joys of power: I want Idame, And, instead of her, a crowd of busy slaves Are ever thronging round me [To his attendants] Hence, away, And guard the city walls; these proud Koreans May think to find us unprepared; already, It seems, they have proclaimed their orphan king; But I'll be duped no longer; he shall die I am distracted with a thousand cares, Dangers, and plots, and foes on every side; Intruding rivals, and a wayward people, Oppress me: when I was a poor unknown I was more happy

SCENE II

Octar, Genghis

Genghis: Well, my friend, you've seen This proud presumptuous Mandarin: what says he?

Octar: He is inflexible; nor threats alarm Nor promises allure him; still he talks Of duty and of virtue, as if we Were vanquished slaves, and he the conqueror I blush to think how we demeaned ourselves, By talking to a wretch, whom by a word We might destroy: let the ungrateful pair Perish together; mutual is their crime, And mutual be their punishment

Genghis: 'Tis strange, That sentiments like these, to us unknown, Should rise in mortal breasts: without a groan, A murmur, or complaint, a father breaks The ties of nature, and would sacrifice His child to please the manes of his sovereign, And the fond wife would die to save her lord The more I see, the more must I admire This wondrous people, great in arts and arms, In learning and in manners great; their kings On wisdom's basis founded all their power; They gave the nations law, by virtue reigned, And governed without conquest; naught hath heaven Bestowed on us but force; our only art Is cruel war; our business to destroy What have I gained by all my victories, By all my guilty laurels stained with blood? The tears, the sighs, the curses of mankind Perhaps, my friend, there is a nobler fame, And worthier of our search: my heart in secret Is jealous of their virtues; I would wish, All conqueror as I am, to imitate The vanquished

Octar: Can you then admire their weakness? What are their boasted arts, the puny offspring Of luxury and vice, that cannot save them From slavery and death? the strong and brave Are born to rule, the feeble to obey: Labor and courage conquer all; but you Tamely submit, a voluntary slave: And must the brave companions of your toil Behold their honor stained, their glory lost, Their king dependent on a woman's smile? Their honest hearts with indignation glow; By me they speak, by me reproach thee, Genghis: Excuse a friend, a fellow soldier, grown Old in thy service; one who cannot bear This amorous sickness of the soul, and longs To guide thy footsteps to the paths of glory

Genghis: Go, fetch Idame

Octar: What, my lord—

Genghis: Obey: Nor dare to murmur; 'tis a subject's part To reverence even the weakness of his master

SCENE III

Genghis: [Alone.] 'Tis not in mortals to resist their fate; She must be mine; what's victory without her? I have made thousands wretched, and am now Myself unhappy: 'midst the venal crowd Of slaves that court my favor, is there one That can relieve the anguish of my soul, Or fill my heart with real bliss? I wanted Some happy error, some delusive joy, To mitigate the sorrows of a king, And lessen the oppressive weight of empire; But Octar, who should heal, hath probed my wounds Too deeply; I have none but monsters round me, Blood-thirsty slaves, unfeeling, merciless, And cruel, disciplined to blood and slaughter: O for a few soft hours of gentle love To brighten this dark scene! they shall not judge, Shall not arraign the conduct of their king: Where is Idame?—ha! she comes

SCENE IV

Genghis, Idame

Idame: My lord, 'Tis cruel to insult a friendless woman, And add fresh weight to her calamities

Genghis: Be not alarmed; your husband yet may live; My vengeance is suspended for a while, And for thy sake I will be merciful: Perhaps it was decreed by heaven Idame Should be reserved to captivate her master, To bend the stubborn fierceness of his nature, And soften his rude heart: you understand me; My laws permit divorce: embrace the offer, And make the sovereign of the world your own I know you love me not, but think what joys Surround a throne; think how thy country's good, Her welfare, and her happiness depend On thy resolve: I know it moves thy wonder To see a haughty conqueror at thy feet: Forget my power, forget my cruelty, Weigh your own interest well, and speak my fate

Idame: I am indeed surprised, and so perhaps Will Genghis be when I shall answer him: There was a time, my lord, you well remember, When he who holds the subject world in awe, This terror of the nations, was no more Than a poor soldier, friendless and unknown; He offered me the pure unspotted heart Of Temugin, and I with pleasure then Would have received it

Genghis: Ha! couldst thou have loved me?

Idame: Perhaps I might; but those to whom I owe My first obedience doomed me to another: Thou knowest the power of parents o'er their children; They are the image of that God we serve, And next to them should be obeyed: this empire Was founded on paternal right, on justice, Honor, and public faith, and holy marriage; And if it be the sacred will of heaven That it must fall a sacrifice to thee, And thy successful crimes, the enlivening spirit That long supported it shall never perish: Your fate has changed; Idame's never can

Genghis: Couldst thou have loved me then?

Idame: I could, my lord, And therefore never must hereafter think On Genghis; I am bound in sacred bonds To Zamti; nay, I'll tell thee more; I love him, Prefer him to the splendor of a throne, And all the honors thou canst lavish on me: Think not it soothes my vanity to spurn A conqueror, all I wish is to fulfil My duty, and do justice to myself: Bestow your favors on some grateful heart, Worthier than mine, that will with joy receive them: May I implore you to conceal from Zamti These proffered terms? 'twould wound his soul to think My truth to him had ever thus been questioned

Genghis: He knows what I expect, and will obey If he desires to live

Idame: He never will: Though cruel torments should extort from him A feigned submission, my firm constancy Would soon recall him to the paths of duty, Of honor, truth, and virtue

Genghis: Can it be, When this ungenerous husband would have given Thy son to death?

Idame: He did: he loved his country: It was a noble crime, and I forgive him: He acted like a hero, and Idame Like the fond mother: even if I had hated I would not have been false to him

Genghis: Amazing! Resistance but inflames my passion for thee, And the more injured, I but love thee more: Yet know, I have a soul that's capable Of rage as well as tenderness

Idame: I know Thou art the master here, and life or death Depend on thee: but tremble at the laws

Genghis: The laws! they are no more, or in my will Alone are to be found; your laws already Have been too fatal to me; they prevented That happy union which my soul desired, And bound thee to another; but they are void, And stand dissolved by my superior power: Obey me, madam, I have given my orders, And I expect your husband should deliver Into my hands the emperor and Idame: Remember, Zamti's life depends on you: Let prudence teach you to disarm the wrath Of an offended king, who, blushing, owns His foolish fondness for a worthless woman

SCENE V

Idame, Asseli

Idame: Thou seest my wretched fate; the tyrant leaves me The cruel choice of infamy or death O, Zamti, I must yield thee to thy fate

Asseli: Rather exert the power which beauty gives thee O'er the proud Scythian, you have found the art To please him

Idame: Would I had not! that, alas! But makes me more unhappy

Asseli: You alone Might soften all the rigor of our fate; For you already his relenting soul Withheld its fierceness; you subdued his rage; Zamti still lives, his rival, and his foe: This bloody conqueror stands in awe of thee, And dare not hurt him: here he first beheld Thy lovely form, here paid his guiltless vows

Idame: No more: it were a crime to think of them

SCENE VI

Zamti, Idame, Asseli

Idame: Zamti! what brought thee hither? what kind power Hath thus restored thee to my arms?

Zamti: The tyrant Hath given me this short respite; by his orders I came to seek thee

Idame: Hast thou heard, my Zamti, The shameful terms proposed to save thy life, And the dear Orphan's?

Zamti: Mine's not worth thy care: What is the loss of one unhappy being Amidst the general ruin? O Idame, Remember my first duty is to save My king; whate'er we boast, whate'er we love, To him we owe it all, except our honor, That only good which we can call our own I have concealed the Orphan 'midst the tombs Of his great ancestors, unless we soon Fly to relieve him, he must perish there Korea's generous prince in vain expects him: Etan, our faithful servant, is in chains; Thou art our only hope; preserve the life Of thy dear infant, and thy husband's honor

Idame: What wouldst thou have me do?

Zamti: Forget me, live But for thy country, give up all to that, And that alone; heaven points out the fair path Of glory to thee, and a husband's death, For Zamti soon must die, shall leave thee free To act as best may serve the common cause: Enslave the Tartar, make him all thy own; And yet to leave thee to that proud usurper Will make the pangs of death more bitter to me: It is a dreadful sacrifice, but duty Spreads sweet content o'er all that she inspires: Idame, be a mother to thy king, And reign; remember, 'tis my last command, Preserve thy sovereign, and be happy

Idame: Stay, Thou knowest me not: thinkest thou I'll ever purchase Those shameful honors with my Zamti's blood? O thou art doubly guilty; love and nature Cry out against thee! barbarous to thy son, And still more cruel to thy wife. O Zamti, Heaven points us out a nobler way to death The tyrant, whether from contempt or love I know not, leaves me at full liberty; I am not watched, or guarded here; I know Each secret path and avenue that leads To the dark tombs where thou hast hid the king; Thither I'll fly, and to Korea's chief Bear the rich prize, the nation's only hope, The royal infant, as a gift from heaven: I know 'twill be in vain, and we must die; But we shall die with glory; we shall leave Behind us names that, worthy of remembrance, shall shine forever in the rolls of time Now, Zamti, have I followed thy example?

Zamti: Thou gracious God, who hast inspired, support her! I blush, my love, at thy superior virtue; Heaven grant thee power to save thy king and country!

ACT V

SCENE I

Idame, Asseli

Asseli: All then is lost; twice in one fatal day Have I beheld thee made a slave: alas! What could a helpless woman unsupported Against a mighty conqueror?

Idame: I have done What duty bade me, carried in my arms The royal infant; for a while his presence Inspired our troops, but Genghis came, and death Followed his steps, the savage herd prevailed, And bore down all before them; I was made Once more a captive

Asseli: Zamti then must perish, And share his master's fate

Idame: They both must die: Perhaps some cruel torments, worse than death, Already are prepared; my son perhaps Must follow them: to triumph o'er my grief, And aggravate my sorrows, the proud tyrant Called me before him: how his looks appalled My shrinking soul, when thrice he lifted up His bloody hand against the wretched infants! Trembling I stepped between, and at his feet Fell prostrate; rudely then he pushed me from him, And turned aside; the savage guards around Seemed waiting for his orders to despatch me

Asseli: He cannot, dare not do it: still, thou seest, Zamti is spared, the orphan king still lives; Let but Idame sue to him for pardon, And all will be forgiven

Idame: O no; his love Is turned to rage; he smiled at my distress, Laughed at my tears, and vowed eternal hatred

Asseli: And yet you may subdue him; the fierce lion Roars in the toils, and bites his chain; he would not Thus talk of hatred if he did not love

Idame: Whether he loves or hates, 'tis time to end This wretched being

Asseli: What have you resolved?

Idame: When heaven hath poured out all its wrath upon us, And filled up the sad measure of our woes, It gives us courage to support our griefs, And suits our strength to our calamities: I feel new force, new vigor in my heart, 'Midst all my sorrows; henceforth I defy The tyrant, and am mistress of my fate

Asseli: But can you leave your child, the dear loved object Of all your hopes and fears?

Idame: There Asseli, You pierce my heart: O dreadful sacrifice! I have done all to save him: the usurper Will not descend so low as to destroy A helpless infant; for his mother's sake, Whom once he loved, perhaps may spare my child; That pleasing hope at least will soothe my soul In the dark hour of death: he will relent When I am gone, nor carry his fierce wrath Beyond the grave, to persecute my son

SCENE II

Idame, Asseli, Octar

Octar: Madam, you must attend the emperor [To the guards] Guard you these infants; watch the door, that none May pass this way [To Asseli] You, madam, may retire

Idame: The emperor send for me?—but I obey Could I have seen my Zamti first! perhaps It is a vain request: does pity never Dwell in a Tartar's breast? might I implore Your friendship to assist me?

Octar: No: when once The royal word is passed, to offer counsel Is little less than treason: you had kings Indeed of old who gave up all their rights, And let their subjects rule; but manners change With times; we listen not to idle prayers, Nor yield to woman's tears; by arms alone We rule the subject world: therefore obey, And wait the emperor's commands

SCENE III

Idame: [Alone.] Thou God Of the afflicted, who beholdest my wrongs, Support me now, inspire me with a portion Of my dear Zamti's courage

SCENE IV

Genghis Khan, Idame

Genghis: Genghis comes Once more to humble thy proud soul; to show thee Thy foul ingratitude, thy base return For all my kindness to thee; yet thou knowest not How guilty thou hast been; thou knowest not yet Thy danger, nor the anguish of my soul; Thou whom I loved and whom I ought to hate, To punish, to destroy

Idame: Then punish me, And me alone; 'tis all I ask of Genghis: Finish a life of misery, satiate here Thy thirst of blood: Idame hath been faithful, That is a crime thou never canst forgive: Strike then, and be revenged

Genghis: Thou knowest I cannot; Thou knowest I am more wretched than thyself; But I'm resolved: the Orphan, and thy son, Are in my power: for Zamti, he has long Deserved to die; the rebel braves my wrath, And yet I spare him; if you wish his life You must forget him; death will break the chain That binds you; then I might with justice seize And make you mine; but know, this proud barbarian, This Scythian tyrant, whom you treat with scorn, Is not unworthy of Idame's love: Abjure your marriage, and I'll raise your child To equal rank and splendor with my own: The orphan shall be safe, your husband spared; Their lives, their welfare, and their happiness, The happiness of Genghis, all depend On thee, Idame; for I love thee still: But think not I will bear thy cruel insults, Thy tyrant scorn, and all the pride of beauty: My soul, thou knowest, is violent; take heed, Provoke it not, least vengeance fall upon thee Speak the decisive word that must determine The fate of Genghis, and his empire; say, Or must I love or hate Idame?

Idame: Neither: Your hatred were unjust, your love most guilty, And most unworthy of us both: I ask Your justice; I demand it; 'tis a debt Which a king owes to all: if you have lost, I would restore it to you, and, in secret, I know your conscience justifies Idame.

Genghis: Then hatred is your choice; 'tis well; henceforth Expect the vengeance of an injured monarch: Your prince, your husband, and your son shall pay For proud Idame's scorn, and with their blood Atone for her ingratitude: their doom Was sealed by thee, thou art their murderer

Idame: Barbarous, inhuman Genghis

Genghis: So I am, Thanks to thy kind regard! you might have had A tender love, but you chose a master Proud, merciless, and savage, one whose hatred Is equal to thy own

Idame: He is my king; As such I reverence him: this single boon, Low on my knees entreat

Genghis: Idame, rise; Speak, I attend: perhaps some kinder thoughts—

Idame: Might Zamti be permitted for a while To visit me in secret?

Genghis: What?

Idame: My lord, But for a moment, 'tis my last request; Perhaps it may be better for us both

Genghis: 'Tis strange: but be it so: perhaps the slave, Taught by calamity, that best of masters, No longer will desire the fatal honor Of being rival to a conqueror: On you his fate depends; divorce, or death: Give him the choice [To Octar] Watch here [To the guards] Guards, follow me: Still am I wavering, still unhappy; still Is Genghis doomed to be the slave of love [Exit]

Idame: [Alone] Once more Idame lives; methinks I feel New strength and vigor shoot through every vein: Now, Genghis, I defy thee!

SCENE V

Zamti, Idame

Idame: O my Zamti, Dearer to me than all those conquerors, Whom servile mortals flatter into gods; My other deity, to whom in vain I never sue: alas, my love, too well Thou knowest our fate; the dreadful hour is come

Zamti: I know it is

Idame: In vain thy patriot care Strove to preserve the orphan king

Zamti: That hope Is lost; we'll think no more on it: thou hast done Thy every duty, and I die content

Idame: What will become of our dear child? forgive A mother, Zamti; I have shown some courage, And therefore thou wilt pardon me

Zamti: The kings Of Cathay are no more; the nobles held In ignominious chains; they most deserve Our pity, who are still condemned to live

Idame: O they have doomed thee to a shameful death

Zamti: 'Tis what I've long expected

Idame: Hear me then; Is there no path to death but from the palace? Bulls bleed at the altar; criminals are dragged To punishment; but generous minds are masters Of their own fate: why meet it from the hands Of Genghis? were we born dependent thus On others' wills? no; let us imitate Our bolder neighbors, live with ease, and die When life grows burdensome: wrongs unrevenged To them are insupportable, and death More welcome far than infamy: they wait not For a proud tyrant's nod, but meet their fate: We've taught these islanders some useful arts, And wherefore deign we not to learn from them Some necessary virtues?—let us die

Zamti: Yes: I approve thy noble resolution, And think, extremity of sorrow mocks The power of laws; but wretched slaves, disarmed As we are, and bowed down beneath our tyrants, Must wait the blow

Idame: [Drawing out a poniard] Strike, Zamti, and be free

Zamti: O heaven!

Idame: Strike here, my Zamti, this weak arm Perhaps might err; thy firmer hand will best Direct the fatal stroke; now sacrifice A faithful wife, and let her husband fall Beside her: yes, my love, we'll die together; With jealous eye the tyrant shall behold us Expiring in each other's arms

Zamti: Thank heaven! Thy virtue never fails; this is the last The dearest mark of my Idame's love; Receive my last farewell; give me the dagger: Now turn aside

Idame: There, take it [Gives him the dagger] Kill me first; Thou tremblest

Zamti: O I cannot

Idame: Strike, my lord

Zamti: I shudder at the thought

Idame: O cruel Zamti, Strike here, and then—

Zamti: I will—now follow me [Attempts to stab himself

Idame: [Laying hold of his arm] You must not—here, my lord—

SCENE VI

Genghis, Octar, Idame

Zamti: Guards

Genghis: O heaven! disarm him [Guards disarm him What would ye do?

Idame: We would have freed ourselves From misery and thee

Zamti: Thou wilt not envy us The privilege to die

Genghis: Indeed I will: O power supreme, thou witness of my wrongs And of my weakness, thou who hast subdued So many kings for me, shall I at last Be worthy of thy goodness?—Zamti, thou Still triumphest o'er me; she whom

I adored, Thy wife, had rather die by thy loved hand Than live with Genghis: but ye both shall learn To bear my yoke, perhaps yet more

Idame: What sayest thou?

Zamti: For what new scene of inhumanity Are we reserved?

Idame: Why is our fate concealed?

Genghis: Be not impatient; ye shall know it soon Ye've done me ample justice, be it mine Now to return it: I admire you both; You have subdued me, and I blush to sit On Cathay's throne, whilst there are souls like yours So much above me; vainly have I tried By glorious deeds to build myself a name Among the nations; you have humbled me, And I would equal you: I did not know That mortals could be masters of themselves; That greatest glory I have learned from you: I am not what I was; to you I owe The wondrous change; I come to reunite, To save, and to protect you: watch, Idame, Your prince's tender years; to thee I give The precious charge, by right of conquest mine; Hereafter I will be a father to him: At length you may confide in Genghis; once I was a conqueror, now I am a king [To Zamti Zamti, be thou our law's interpreter, And make the world as good and pure as thou art; Teach reason, justice, and morality, And let the conquered rule the conquerors; Let wisdom reign, and still direct our valor; Let prudence triumph over strength; her king Will set the example, and your conqueror Henceforth shall be obedient to your law

Idame: What do I hear?

Zamti: Thou art indeed our king, And we shall bless thy sway

Idame: What could inspire This great design, and work this change?

Genghis: Thy virtues

End.